INVESTIGATING SCIENCE CHALLENGES

Investigating MAGNETISM

Richard Spilsbury

CRABTREE
PUBLISHING COMPANY
WWW.CRABTREEBOOKS.COM

Author: Richard Spilsbury

Editors: Sarah Eason, Jennifer Sanderson, Petrice Custance, Reagan Miller

Proofreaders: Kris Hirschmann, Janine Deschenes

Indexer: Wendy Scavuzzo

Editorial director: Kathy Middleton

Design: Emma DeBanks

Cover design and additional artwork: Emma DeBanks

Photo research: Rachel Blount

Production coordinator and prepress technician: Tammy McGarr

Print coordinator: Katherine Berti

Consultant: David Hawksett

Produced for Crabtree Publishing Company by Calcium Creative

Photo Credits:

t=Top, tr=Top Right, tl=Top Left

Inside: Shutterstock: Alphaspirit: p. 20; BkkPixel: p. 21; Dar1930: p. 19t; Drohn: pp. 1, 26-27; DW labs Incorporated: p. 6; FotoCuisinette: p. 4; India Picture: p. 12; Daniel Jedzura: p. 9; Vasin Lee: p. 7; Martin Novak: p. 13; Ivan Smuk: p. 15t; Thanamat Somwan: p. 25r; Manfred Steinbach: pp. 24-25; Dmytro Vietrov: pp. 14-15; Marian Weyo: p. 5; YK: pp. 18-19.

Cover: Tudor Photography.

Library and Archives Canada Cataloguing in Publication

Spilsbury, Richard, 1963-, author
    Investigating magnetism / Richard Spilsbury.

(Investigating science challenges)
Includes index.
Issued in print and electronic formats.
ISBN 978-0-7787-4208-1 (hardcover).--
ISBN 978-0-7787-4312-5 (softcover).--
ISBN 978-1-4271-2012-0 (HTML)

    1. Magnetism--Juvenile literature. I. Title.

QC753.7.S65 2018   j538   C2017-907742-2
                                            C2017-907743-0

Library of Congress Cataloging-in-Publication Data

Names: Spilsbury, Richard, 1963- author.
Title: Investigating magnetism / Richard Spilsbury.
Description: New York, New York : Crabtree Publishing Company, [2018] | Series: Investigating science challenges | Includes index.
Identifiers: LCCN 2017059670 (print) | LCCN 2017060086 (ebook) | ISBN 9781427120120 (Electronic HTML) | ISBN 9780778742081 (reinforced library binding) | ISBN 9780778743125 (pbk.)
Subjects: LCSH: Magnetism--Juvenile literature.
Classification: LCC QC753.7 (ebook) | LCC QC753.7 .S65 2018 (print) | DDC 538--dc23
LC record available at https://lccn.loc.gov/2017059670

Crabtree Publishing Company

www.crabtreebooks.com   1-800-387-7650

Printed in the U.S.A./022018/CG20171220

Published in Canada
Crabtree Publishing
616 Welland Ave.
St. Catharines, Ontario
L2M 5V6

Published in the United States
Crabtree Publishing
PMB 59051
350 Fifth Avenue, 59th Floor
New York, New York 10118

Published in the United Kingdom
Crabtree Publishing
Maritime House
Basin Road North, Hove
BN41 1WR

Published in Australia
Crabtree Publishing
3 Charles Street
Coburg North
VIC, 3058

CONTENTS

MAGNETISM IS A FORCE

People have known about magnets for thousands of years. The first magnet discovered in ancient times was a type of rock. It was named "magnetite," from which comes the word "magnet." In ancient China, people first used magnets to make **compasses** to help them find their way, because magnets will naturally point north. Long ago, magnetism must have seemed like magic, but science investigations have helped us understand how magnetism and magnets work.

Hold a magnet close to a refrigerator door and you will feel the magnetic **force** pulling the object toward it.

Using Magnetism

Most of us use magnetism every day without even realizing it is there. For example, magnets help refrigerator doors stay closed. Anything with an **electric motor** in it, from an electric toothbrush to an electric car, uses magnets to turn **electricity** into motion, or movement. Magnetism is a kind of force. A force is a push or a pull on an object. It happens when two objects interact, or when one object does something to another object.

The Effects of Magnetism

Have you played with magnets and discovered how they pull together and stick to each other? You have probably seen that magnetic forces can pull magnets toward some kinds of metal. For example, a magnet can pull on steel paper clips to lift them up. A magnet can also push on another magnet to make it jump or slide away.

Giant magnets can be used to lift and move large, heavy steel objects quickly and easily.

INVESTIGATE

Scientists **observe** the world around them and ask questions. They then plan and carry out **investigations** to find answers. In this book, you will carry out investigations to answer questions about magnetism. On pages 28 and 29, you can find investigation tips, check your work, and read suggestions for other investigations you can try.

HOW MAGNETS WORK

Magnets come in a variety of sizes and shapes, such as bars, rings, or horseshoes. All magnets are made from materials that produce a magnetic force which runs all the way through it. This force is strongest near the ends of a magnet, which are called the **poles**. One end of a magnet is a north pole, while the opposite end is a south pole. If you cut a bar magnet in half, you would create two smaller magnets, each with its own north and south poles.

One flat side, or face, of a ring magnet is the north pole. The opposite face is the south pole

Attraction and Repulsion

Unlike, or different, poles **attract** each other. So, if you put the south pole of one magnet near the north pole of another magnet, magnetic forces pull them together. Poles that are the same **repel** each other. This means if you try to put two north or two south poles together, the magnets will push away from each other.

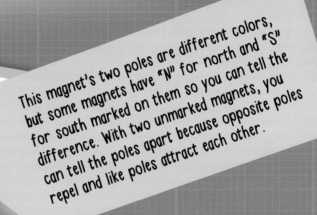

This magnet's two poles are different colors, but some magnets have "N" for north and "S" for south marked on them so you can tell the difference. With two unmarked magnets, you can tell the poles apart because opposite poles repel and like poles attract each other.

An Invisible Force

One of the most interesting things about magnets is the way they can attract other magnets or other **magnetic materials** from a distance. When we want to move something, we have to touch it or make contact with it, such as when we kick a ball or lift an object. Magnetic forces can move things without touching them. Some magnets are stronger than others and can attract or repel more powerfully than weak magnets. That is why some magnets start working at a greater distance from an object than others.

MAGNETIC FIELDS

The invisible area of magnetism all around a magnet is called its **magnetic field**. Magnetic fields fill the space around a magnet where the magnetic forces work. If something is placed within an object's magnetic field, it will be attracted or repelled. These effects happen along field lines. Field lines begin and end at the magnetic north and south poles.

If you drop **iron** filings (tiny pieces of iron) around a magnet, you can see them line up along the magnet's field lines.

Natural Magnetic Fields

Earth behaves like a gigantic magnet because its core, or center, is made up of melted metals, including a lot of magnetic materials, such as iron. Like other magnets, Earth has its own enormous magnetic field. Earth's magnetic field reaches into space, in an invisible area called the **magnetosphere**. Like smaller magnetic fields, the magnetosphere can affect things around it. For example, the magnetosphere repels tiny, fast-moving **particles** from space so they do not reach Earth. These particles could cause dangerous health problems, such as cancer.

Magnetic Compasses

Compasses contain magnets. If you hang a bar magnet from a string, its north pole will always try to point toward Earth's North Pole. That is why a magnet's north pole is called the north-seeking pole. Since the north-seeking pole of a magnet always wants to point north, magnets can be used inside a compass to help people find their way.

Particles from the Sun that interact with Earth's magnetic field can create light displays, called **auroras**, in the sky. These spectacular displays are usually seen near Earth's magnetic poles. This is because the planet's magnetic field bends inward and is most powerful at these points.

INVESTIGATE

On a magnetic noteboard, paper notes can stick to metal using magnets. This is proof that magnetic forces operate through paper. Magnetic fields can go through many solid materials, but it depends on the thickness of the materials. Would a magnetic field feel stronger through cardboard or paper? Is there a limit to the number of sheets of paper that can stick to a noteboard with a single magnet? Does the magnet's strength make a difference?

9

WORKING AT A DISTANCE

The force of a magnet on something made of metal, such as steel paper clips, acts over a distance known as its magnetic field. The stronger the magnet, the greater its magnetic field. How can you discover how far a magnet's magnetic field reaches? Let's investigate magnetic fields.

You Will Need:
- A clothespin
- A paper cup
- Masking tape
- A strong bar magnet
- Steel paper clips
- A pencil
- A sheet of paper

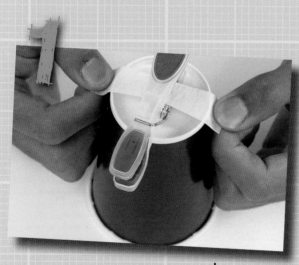

Step 1: Attach the bottom leg of the clothespin to the top of the overturned cup using tape.

Step 2: Grip the magnet between the clothespin's "jaws." Fold open one paper clip to make a hook, and touch it to the magnet. Add more paper clips, one by one, to the hook. How many paper clips can you add before the hook falls off? Use words and pictures to record your result.

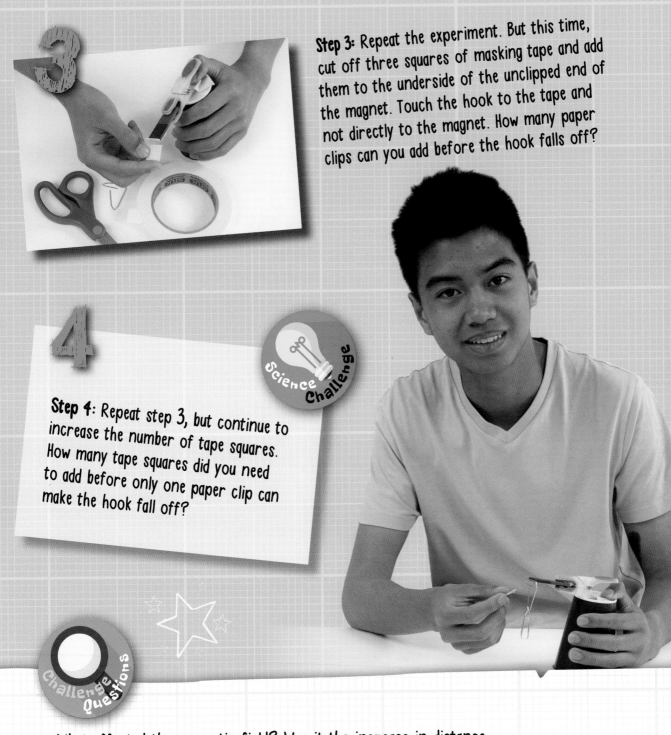

Step 3: Repeat the experiment. But this time, cut off three squares of masking tape and add them to the underside of the unclipped end of the magnet. Touch the hook to the tape and not directly to the magnet. How many paper clips can you add before the hook falls off?

Step 4: Repeat step 3, but continue to increase the number of tape squares. How many tape squares did you need to add before only one paper clip can make the hook fall off?

Science Challenge

Challenge Questions

- What affected the magnetic field? Was it the increase in distance between the magnet and the paper clips? Or was it the material from which the tape is made?
- Does the magnetic field change size during step 4?
- Why is it important to use paper clips that are the same size?

MAGNETIC MATERIALS

Magnetic materials are substances that are attracted to magnets. Magnetic materials are always metals. Nonmetallic materials, such as paper, wood, plastic, concrete, glass, and textiles, are never magnetic. They are called nonmagnetic. Although all magnetic materials are metals, only a few metals are truly magnetic.

Which Materials Are Magnetic?

The most common magnetic material is iron. Any metal that contains iron will be attracted to a magnet. A metal made from a mixture of different metals is called an **alloy**. Steel is an alloy that contains up to about 80 percent iron. This is why steel objects, such as paper clips, are attracted to magnets. Other magnetic metals include nickel and cobalt. Most other common metals, such as copper, gold, silver, aluminum, brass, and lead, are not magnetic. An aluminum pop can, for example, will not be attracted to a magnet.

At recycling plants, workers can use magnets to separate iron and steel, which are magnetic materials, from aluminum waste, which is not.

REGULATOR-CETRISA

Strong and Weak Magnets

People mix metal alloys to create different strengths of magnets. The strongest magnets are alloys made from rare-earth metals, which are a group of 17 **elements** that are heavier than iron. Other strong magnets are made with ferrite. Ferrite is an alloy made of iron, oxygen, and other elements. Ferrite magnets are also known as ceramic magnets, and can be found on the back of fridge magnets. Ferrite is designed to be cheap and resistant to heat and rust, which makes it last longer. Another powerful and long-lasting magnet is made from alnico, an alloy named after its main components: aluminum, nickel, and cobalt.

Our bodies need iron to keep our blood healthy, so some breakfast cereals are **fortified** with iron. You can check if your cereal has iron in it by grinding some of it into a powder and waving a strong magnet near it!

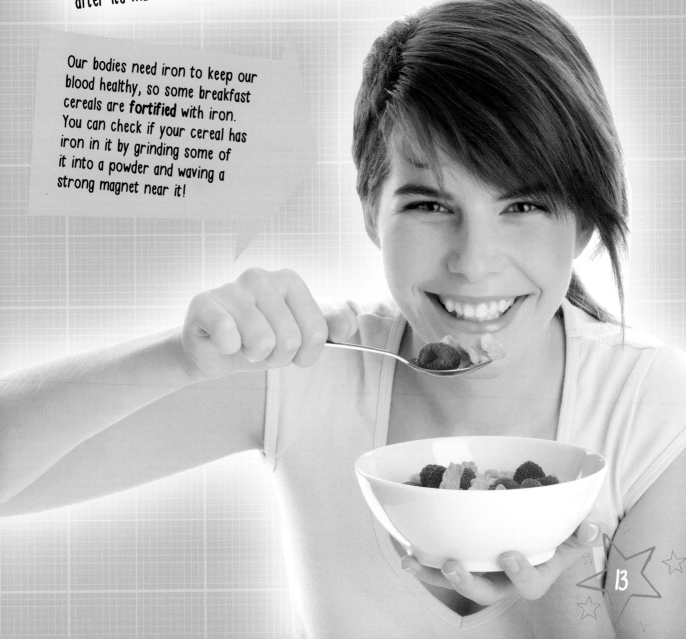

13

MAKING MAGNETS

A permanent magnet is a solid material that produces its own consistent magnetic field. Magnetic materials can become temporarily **magnetized** by a transfer of magnetic **energy**.

The Energy Inside Magnets

The secret to whether material is magnetic lies in its **atoms**. Everything that exists is made up of atoms. The center of each atom is called a **nucleus**. Around a nucleus are **electrons**, which are electrically **charged**. Electrons whiz around the nucleus producing a weak magnetic field. In nonmagnetic materials, these magnetic fields point in different directions, so they cancel one another out. In magnets, the fields line up and point in the same direction. Together they create a strong magnetic force.

The tiny fields in the atoms of a magnet are arranged neatly in the same direction, like the cars in this parking lot. How would the parked cars look if they were arranged like the tiny fields in a nonmagnetic material?

14

Transferring Energy

Magnetism is a kind of energy. Energy is the ability to do work and it can be moved or transferred from one place to another. If you run a magnet a few times over certain metal objects, such as an iron nail, you can transfer magnetic energy to it. This will turn the material into a temporary magnet. This happens because the magnet pulls and lines up some of the magnetic fields inside the iron nail in the same direction, which magnetizes the material.

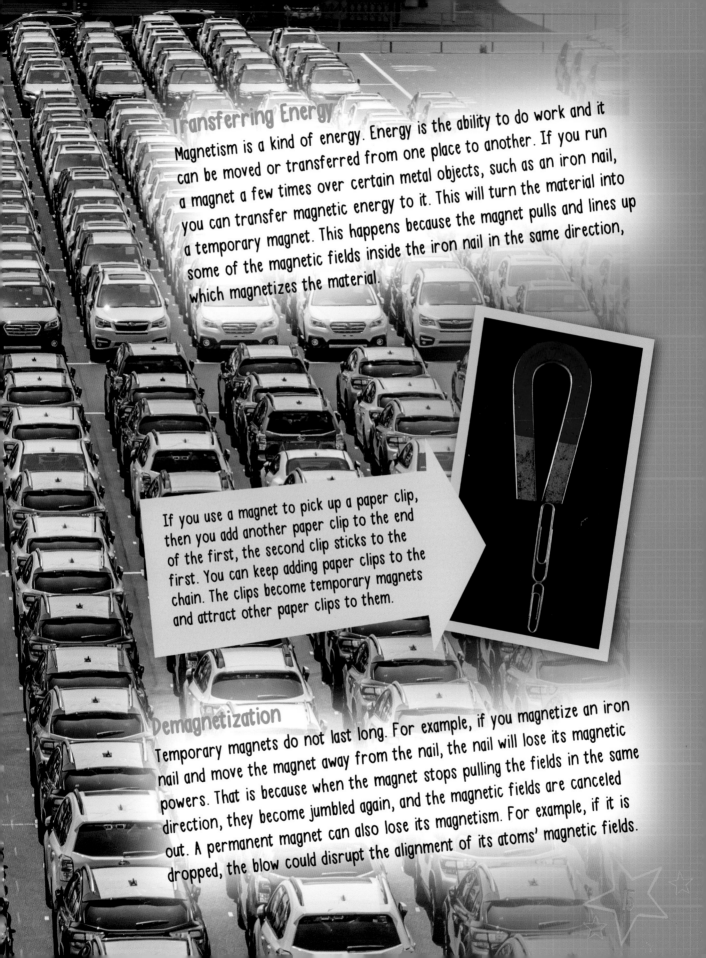

If you use a magnet to pick up a paper clip, then you add another paper clip to the end of the first, the second clip sticks to the first. You can keep adding paper clips to the chain. The clips become temporary magnets and attract other paper clips to them.

Demagnetization

Temporary magnets do not last long. For example, if you magnetize an iron nail and move the magnet away from the nail, the nail will lose its magnetic powers. That is because when the magnet stops pulling the fields in the same direction, they become jumbled again, and the magnetic fields are canceled out. A permanent magnet can also lose its magnetism. For example, if it is dropped, the blow could disrupt the alignment of its atoms' magnetic fields.

ELECTROMAGNETS

Magnetism and electricity are closely related. Attraction and repulsion are caused by electrons moving in atoms of magnetic materials, and an electric **current** is the flow of electrons. The flow of electricity can create a magnetic field. The interaction between magnetism and electricity is called **electromagnetism**.

The coils in electromagnets are often formed from dozens of loops of very thin copper wire.

Making Electromagnets

An electromagnet is a magnet that is created and controlled by the flow of electricity. An electromagnet is often made up of a copper wire, looped many times into a **cylindrical** coil. When electricity flows around this coil, a magnetic field is created. If an iron bar is placed inside the coil of wire, the electric current magnetizes the iron bar, but only temporarily. When the electricity is turned off and the electric current no longer flows through the wire, the iron bar loses its magnetism.

Using Electromagnets

Electromagnets are widely used in many devices, including motors and headphones. They can be turned on and off by switching the electricity supply on and off, so they are magnetic only when needed. It is also possible to make electromagnets instantly weaker or stronger by decreasing or increasing the electric current being passed through the wire. This means people can make a stronger magnetic field in an electromagnet than a permanent magnet of the same size.

In a junkyard, a crane lowers a large iron disc into a pile of scrap iron and steel. When the operator switches on the electricity, the disc becomes a powerful electromagnet that attracts the scrap steel and lifts it elsewhere.

INVESTIGATE

A junkyard electromagnet is powerful enough to lift tons of steel because of the way it is built. The strength of any electromagnet depends partly on the number of times a wire is coiled around it. Why is this? Would you expect a stronger electromagnet to have more loops of wire than a weaker one?

Let's Investigate

ELECTROMAGNETIC CHALLENGE

When an electric current flows through a wire, it creates a magnetic field around the wire. The more wire that is coiled in an electromagnet, the greater the size and power of its magnetic field. Let's investigate how the number of coils affects the strength of the electromagnet.

Safety Note
Never use other sizes of batteries. They could be dangerous.

Step 1: Wind the wire 10 times around the nail without overlapping the wire.

Step 2: With the help of an adult, use the wire cutters to remove 1 inch (2.5 cm) of plastic coating from each end of the wire. Tape one end of the wire to one end of the battery and the other end of the wire to the other end of the battery.

18

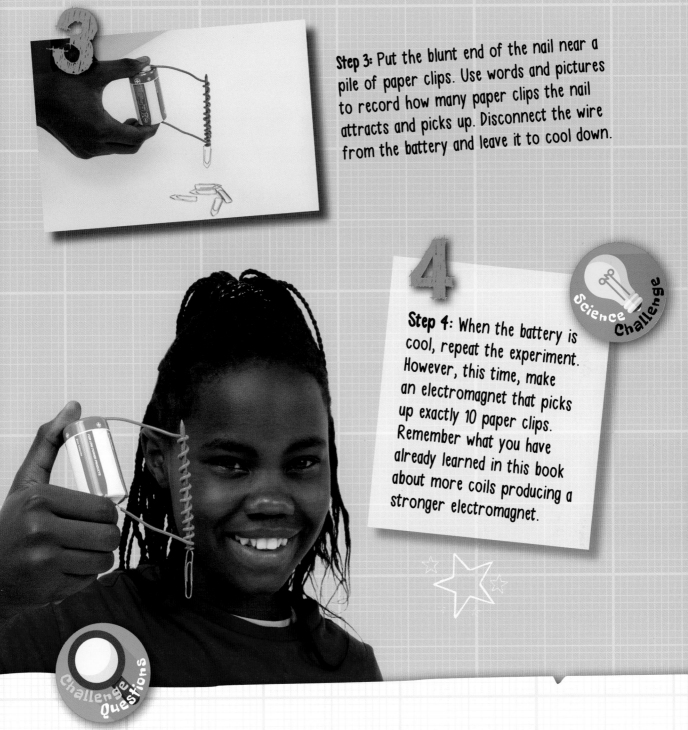

Step 3: Put the blunt end of the nail near a pile of paper clips. Use words and pictures to record how many paper clips the nail attracts and picks up. Disconnect the wire from the battery and leave it to cool down.

Step 4: When the battery is cool, repeat the experiment. However, this time, make an electromagnet that picks up exactly 10 paper clips. Remember what you have already learned in this book about more coils producing a stronger electromagnet.

Science Challenge

Challenge Questions

- What was the difference in the number of coils between the electromagnets in steps 1 and 4?
- If you could not pick up exactly 10 paper clips, why do you think this was?
- Why is it important to put the blunt end of the nail the same distance from a pile of paper clips each time? How does this help to make it a fair test?

MACHINES USING MAGNETS

Do you know what hair dryers, vacuum cleaners, electric drills, and food mixers have in common? They are all machines that use magnetic forces in their electric motors to convert electrical energy into movement energy.

Electric Motors

Electric motors contain an electromagnet inside a permanent magnet. The electric current flows one way, then the other, through the wires in the electromagnet. This makes its magnetic field alternately push and pull against the poles of the permanent magnet. It makes the electromagnet spin around and around, as long as the current keeps flowing. That spinning motion can turn a drill to make holes in materials, a paddle to beat cake batter, a fan to blow warm air from a hair dryer, or a vacuum cleaner to suck up dust.

Making Power

Electricity can be used to make magnets, and the movement of a magnet can produce electricity. If a magnet is moved quickly through a coil of copper wire, its magnetic field pulls electrons so they flow between atoms in the wire. This produces an electric current. You can turn the handle on a wind-up radio or flashlight to spin a magnet through coiled wires that produce power to make sound or light.

The magnets in an electric motor cause a sharp tool, called a drill bit, clamped in the end of the drill to spin very fast and cut holes.

Power Plants

The large amounts of power we need to operate lights, computers, washing machines, and other electrical appliances mostly comes from **generators** in power plants. In a generator, a massive coil of copper wire spins inside huge magnets to create an electrical current. The generator is attached to a giant fan called a **turbine** that creates the spinning motion by using moving steam, wind, or water.

Hair dryers heat up air and a motorized fan blows that warm air out to dry your hair.

MAGNETS ON THE MOVE

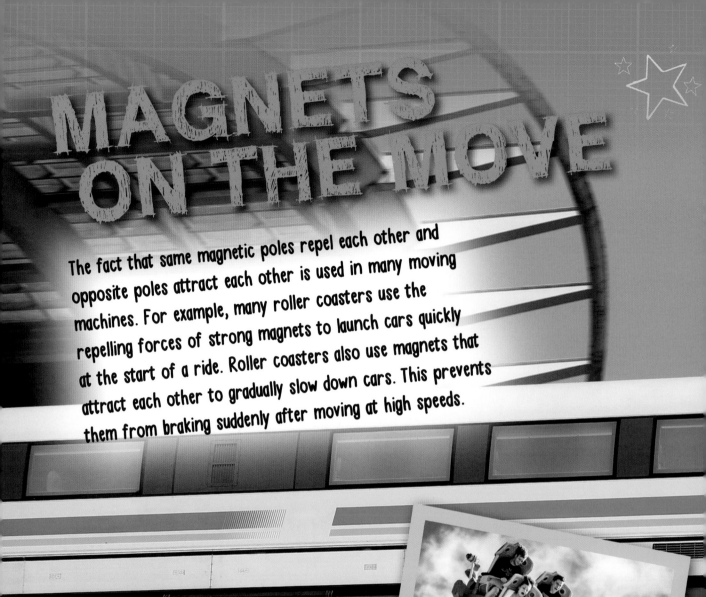

The fact that same magnetic poles repel each other and opposite poles attract each other is used in many moving machines. For example, many roller coasters use the repelling forces of strong magnets to launch cars quickly at the start of a ride. Roller coasters also use magnets that attract each other to gradually slow down cars. This prevents them from braking suddenly after moving at high speeds.

Using the repelling power of magnets, some roller-coaster cars can be launched forward at speeds of up to 60 miles (100 km) per hour in just seconds!

Maglev Trains

Maglev is short for magnetic **levitation**. Maglev trains have magnets on their undersides. They run on tracks that contain coils of magnetized wire. The repelling and attracting forces created by these magnetic forces lift the train so it levitates, or floats, slightly above the track. Maglev trains also use electromagnets to propel themselves forward. Magnets ahead of the train are paired with opposite magnetic poles on the train, to pull the train forward. Magnets with magnetic poles facing the same direction as those on the train push it from the back.

Most trains are slowed by the force of **friction** as their wheels rub against the rail tracks. A maglev train avoids friction by floating, allowing it to reach speeds of up to 375 miles (603 km) per hour.

INVESTIGATE

The magnets that lift a heavy train have to be very powerful. However, you can levitate a pencil using much smaller magnets. How would you arrange the magnets on the pencil and those on a base for it to float? What shapes of magnet would you use to make the pencil spin while levitating?

Let's Investigate

FLOATING PENCIL

Magnetic forces can make things move apart because like poles repel. Have you noticed how magnets with like poles push things upward or away when you move them closer together? Let's investigate how these forces make things levitate, or float.

THINK!

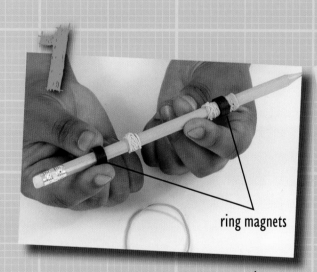

ring magnets

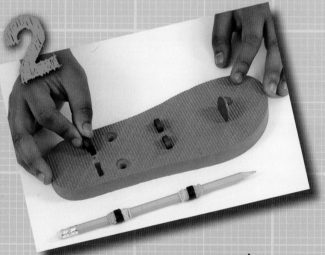

Step 1: Slide two of the ring magnets onto the pencil, with the poles facing the same way. Use rubber bands to attach the magnets in position, so the pencil is divided into three equal parts.

Step 2: Ask an adult to help you cut five slits in the base of the flip-flop as shown above. Push the coin into the slit at the top end, and one ring magnet into each of the other four slits, with poles facing the same way as those on the pencil.

24

Step 3: What happens when you place the pencil above the magnets in the flip-flop with the pencil's sharp end touching the coin?

Step 4: Now remove one of the magnets from the flip-flop and repeat the experiment. Can you make the pencil levitate? Remember what you have already learned in this book about the way magnets repel and attract.

Science Challenge

Challenge Questions

- To make the pencil levitate, is the position and direction of the poles on the magnets important? If so, why?
- When the pencil levitates, is it the result of magnets attracting or repelling?
- Did your pencil levitate with a magnet removed?
- What effect will using more magnets have on the pencil?

25

INVESTIGATE MORE

Magnetism is a fantastic, invisible force produced by magnets. We can experience a magnet's force when its field repels or attracts other magnets or metal objects. Magnets range from the small ones used to close fridge doors to powerful electromagnets that can lift massive trains.

Magnets in Machines

Magnets are important in many machines. Anything with an electric motor, from the fan in a computer to an electric bus, uses the repelling properties of magnets to produce movement. Most of our power comes from big generators in power stations. Those generators spin a coil of wire inside magnets to create electricity.

Magnets are also important in recording and playing sound. In a microphone, the sound waves moving through air are used to move a coil of wire past a magnet. This movement produces patterns of electric current, and loudspeakers then convert these patterns back into sounds! Try doing some research on your own. How do car horns, door bells, and guitar pickups use electromagnets to help make sounds?

Magnetic fields act through layers of paper, but did you know they can also be used to see through a person's body? **MRI** scanners are widely used in health care.

Magnets for Navigation

Earth's natural magnetic field has been used for thousands of years by people to help navigate their way. Did you know that there are other animals that also detect magnetism in order to find their way? Research how magnetism helps sea turtles and monarch butterflies migrate, or make long journeys between particular places each year, and why these animals migrate.

INVESTIGATE

What else would you like to discover about magnets? Computer hard drives and bank cards store information because materials on them are magnetized using electromagnets. The strip on the back of a bank card is made up of tiny magnetic pieces. Can you find out how this works? You could also discover why people are careful not to bring a magnet too close to their hard drives and credit cards.

27

Science Challenge TIPS

Pages 10-11: Working at a Distance

You should find that the magnetic field is affected by the number of pieces of tape. The more tape pieces that are added, the greater the distance between the magnet and the paper clips. With more and more layers of tape, it can hold fewer and fewer clips because the stacked tape moves the paper clip farther from the magnet and toward the outer edges of the magnet's field, where the force of attraction is much weaker. Eventually, the weight of just one paper clip can pull the hook from the magnet. This is because as the magnetic force gets gradually weaker, the amount of weight the magnet can hold is reduced. The paper material making the tape has no direct impact on this field.

The magnetic field does not change size. Any magnet's magnetic field is fixed in size and shape. Using paper clips that are the same size ensures that the test is fair and accurate.

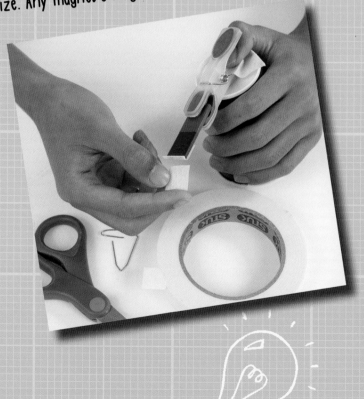

Why not try the test again using different materials in place of the tape? To make the test fair, use pieces of other material that are roughly the same size and thickness as the tape.

Pages 18-19: Electromagnetic Challenge

The nail has a stronger temporary magnetic field for each extra coil of wire around it when the battery is attached. This is because the small magnetic field in each coil is multiplied by the number of coils. The exact number of coils to lift 10 paper clips depends on the weight of each paper clip and the width of the nail. If you cannot pick up 10 paper clips, you need to make a stronger electromagnet. What could you do to increase the strength of your electromagnet? Would you need to adjust the length of the nail or the number of coils, or both? Give reasons for your answer.

Pages 24-25: Floating Pencil

The pencil will float only if the magnets are positioned side by side, not too close together, with the pencil between them. It floats as a result of the magnets repelling. The position and direction of the poles are important because they determine whether the magnets attract or repel.

The pencil floats because the magnets' fields, pushing from two different points, combine to firmly hold the pencil. If you remove a magnet, the pencil becomes unstable and will fall down because its magnetic field gets pushed to one side by the magnetic field on the flip-flop. If you use more magnets, the pencil will float higher because the magnetic fields are stronger.

To further investigate, try spinning the pencil by twisting one end of it. It should keep spinning for a while. Remembering what you learned about maglev trains, why do you think it spins like this?

29

GLOSSARY

Some bold-faced words are defined where they appear in the text.

atoms The tiny particles that make up everything. Atoms are so small that we cannot see them.

attract Pull closer together

auroras The light displays caused by the effects of Earth's magnetic field on charged particles in space

charged Describes something that has more or fewer electrons than normal

compasses Instruments with a magnetized pointer used to detect Earth's North Pole

current The flow of electrons from one place to another

cylindrical Describes a shape with straight sides, and circular in cross-section; having the form of a cylinder

electric motor A device that produces movement using spinning of an electromagnet inside a permanent magnet

electricity A form of energy that is used to power most of the machines people use every day

electromagnetism The interaction between magnetism and electricity

electrons The very small parts of an atom that have a negative electric charge

elements The simplest chemical substances including carbon, oxygen, and iron

energy Ability or power to do work

force The effect that causes things to move in a particular way, usually a push or a pull

fortified Enriched or made stronger; a fortified food has nutrients added to it

friction The action of one object or surface moving across another. Friction is a force that can slow things down.

generators Machines that make electricity

investigations Procedures carried out to observe, study, or test something to learn more about it

iron A type of metal found in Earth, widely used to make tough steel

levitation When something rises and floats in the air

magnetic field The invisible area around a magnet or electromagnet in which the force of magnetism acts

magnetic materials Metals that are attracted to magnets

magnetized When something has been made magnetic

magnetosphere The region of space into which Earth's magnetic field stretches

MRI The acronym for magnetic resonance imaging. MRI is used to take an image of the inside of a person's body.

observe To use your senses to gather information

particles Extremely tiny pieces of material

poles The two points on a magnet, often the ends, that have opposing magnetic qualities

repel Push farther apart

turbines Machines with blades that are turned, for example by the push of steam, water, or wind, usually to operate a generator

LEARNING MORE

Find out more about magnetism and its uses.

Books

Arbuthnott, Gill. *Your Guide to Electricity and Magnetism* (Drawn to Science: Illustrated Guides to Key Science Concepts). Crabtree Publishing Company, 2017.

Forest, Christopher. *Focus on Magnetism* (Hands-On STEM). North Star Editions, 2017.

Gardner, Robert. *Experiments with Electricity and Magnetism* (Science Whiz Experiments). Enslow Publishing, 2017.

Hagler, Gina, and John Willis. *Magnets* (Do-It-Yourself Experiments). Weigl, 2016.

Websites

Learn more about magnetism at:
www.explainthatstuff.com/magnetism.html

Discover amazing facts about magnets at:
www.physics4kids.com/files/elec_magneticfield.html

Find out more about magnetic forces at:
www.nationalgeographic.org/encyclopedia/magnetism

INDEX

About the AUTHOR

Richard Spilsbury has a science degree, and has had a lifelong fascination with science. He has written and co-written many books for young people on a wide variety of topics, from ants to avalanches.